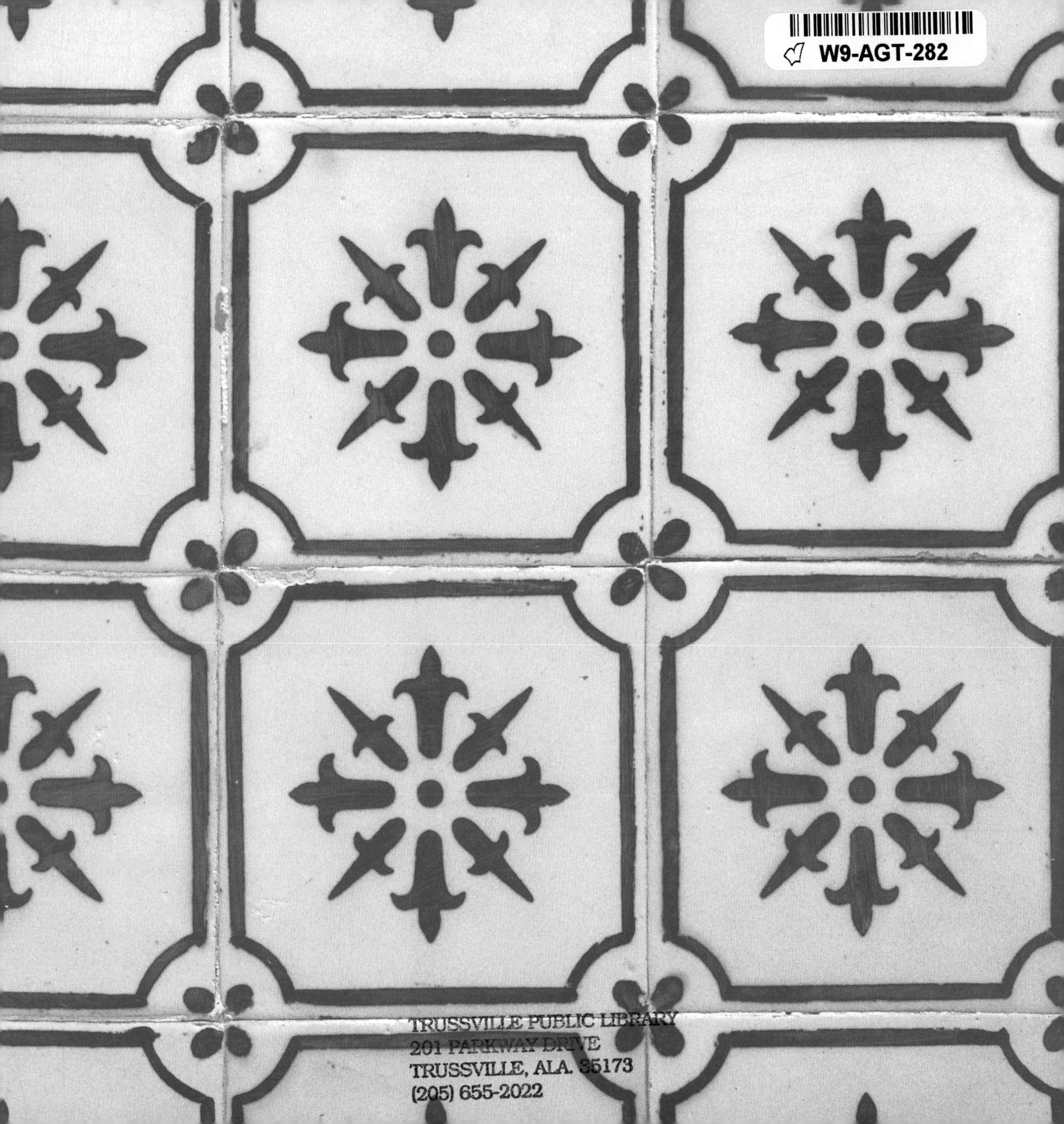

MONET'S HOUSE

MONET'S HOUSE

An Impressionist Interior

HEIDE MICHELS

Photographs by
GUY BOUCHET

Translation by
HELEN IVOR

CLARKSON POTTER/PUBLISHERS
NEW YORK

A Maxim, mon fils

Originally published in Great Britain in 1997 by
Frances Lincoln Limited, London.

Published by Clarkson N. Potter/Publishers,
201 East 50th Street, New York New York 10022.
Member of the Crown Publishing Group.

http://www.randomhouse.com/

CLARKSON N. POTTER, POTTER,
and colophon are trademarks of Clarkson N. Potter, Inc.

Printed in Hong Kong

Library of Congress Cataloging-in-publication data is
available on request.

ISBN 0-517-70667-9

10 9 8 7 6 5 4 3 2 1

First American Edition

FRONTISPIECE: *Claude Monet photographed at the door of
his second studio in 1905.* TITLE PAGE: *The dining room.*
RIGHT: *Monet's desk in the studio drawing room.*
FAR RIGHT: *The roll-top desk in Monet's bedroom.*

Contents

A House In The Country

F ew painters have come to be so closely identified with their homes as Claude Monet is with Giverny. The forty-three years he spent there represent exactly half his life; and the surrounding countryside, and the flower and water gardens he made, inspired much of his greatest work. Monet's sensitivity to light and color also infused the interior of the house, which was boldly but simply decorated to provide a perfect backdrop to the life of his extended family and a harmonious place to entertain friends.

Throughout his life Claude Monet was attracted to water; he never tired of following the River Seine as it flowed northwest from Paris to its estuary at Le Havre, the town where he had spent his childhood. He painted its ever-changing moods and the ever-changing skies above as it flowed chaotically along its course through Argenteuil, Vétheuil, Poissy, Vernon, and Rouen toward the coast. These were all places where he lived at various times during his career, and it was perhaps inevitable that he should make his permanent home in the Seine valley, in the little village of Giverny.

Monet set up home in Giverny in 1883 with Alice Hoschedé, a married mother of six children: Blanche, Germaine, Suzanne, Marthe, Jean-Pierre, and Jacques. The Monets and the Hoschedés had started sharing a house five years before, when Monet's first wife Camille was alive and Ernest Hoschedé still living with his wife. According to Blanche, the two families

Monet painted this intense and introspective portrait of himself in a painter's smock and beret in 1886, three years after his arrival at Giverny.

were already very close and often met in Monet's studio or in Monceau Park in Paris. As a wealthy textile manufacturer and part-owner of a Paris department store, Ernest owned a collection of avant-garde art that included several paintings by Monet, and he commissioned four large canvases from him for the oval salon of his eighteenth-century chateau of Rottembourg, at Montgeron near Paris. He had a particular liking for the Impressionists, and he and Alice regularly played host to Manet, Renoir, and Sisley, as well as to many musicians and writers. Yet his apparent prosperity did not last. Ernest made several bad investments and in the spring of 1878 was declared bankrupt. The chateau was sold, the furniture seized to pay his debts, and his art collection dispersed. After enjoying a life of affluence and lavish entertaining, Alice's world collapsed.

Monet, too, was in financial straits, struggling to make a living from his painting. In 1873, dissatisfied with the available opportunities to show their work, a number of artists, including Monet, Camille Pissarro, Edgar Degas, Auguste Renoir, Berthe Morisot, and Alfred Sisley, had formed a society

devoted to exhibiting their paintings independently. Their first exhibition opened in April the following year in the Paris studio of the renowned photographer Félix Nadar. Among the canvases on display was a view of the docks in Le Havre by Monet, to which he had given the title *Impression, Sunrise*. Using the word "impression" as the basis for a series of derogatory remarks about the whole exhibition, the critic Louis Leroy wrote an article in which he applied the term Impressionist to the whole group.

Following their first exhibition, the Impressionists organized a sale at the Drouot auction rooms in April 1875, but Monet's canvases only fetched between 165 and 375 francs, and the other artists fared little better. A second exhibition at Durand-Ruel's gallery was greeted with a chorus of boos and jeers by the press. One of the most outspoken critics, Albert Wolff, wrote in *Le Figaro*: "These so-called artists who call themselves the Uncompromising, or the Impressionists, they take a canvas, some paint and brushes, fling a few colors about at random, then sign the result ... What an appalling example of human vanity taken to the pitch of insanity."

The tide of public opinion gradually began to turn in favor of Impressionism, and Monet found support among discerning critics such as Octave Mirbeau, who wrote: "We are overcome by the impression that … art, as it were, disappears, slips away, and we are no longer looking at a painting but at living nature captured and tamed by this miraculous painter." He also received encouragement from his dealer Paul Durand-Ruel, who became father-figure, advisor, and banker to many Impressionist artists, helped to organize their exhibitions, and did his best to persuade his clients to buy their work.

But the improvement in critical reception did not make an immediate difference to Monet's material existence. Some Impressionist painters had other sources of income. Manet and Degas, for example, had private means, while Cézanne's father gave him a small allowance. Following his introduction to Mme Charpentier, who kept a fashionable salon, Renoir had begun to make a living as a society portraitist. Monet, however, relied almost entirely on the paintings created on his own initiative to keep his family. He had always lived beyond his means, so in 1878, when the opportunity arose to save money by moving in with the Hoschedés in the riverside village of Vétheuil, it seemed worth trying.

Yet life in Vétheuil was not easy. A year after the Monets and Hoschedés arrived there, Camille Monet died, leaving two small sons, Jean and Michel. Ernest Hoschedé, whose behavior following his bankruptcy had been erratic to say the least, spent more and more of his time in Paris. Eventually in the autumn of 1881, Monet asked Alice if she would move with him to Poissy, a town on the Seine about 20 kilometres from Paris, where he was planning to rent a house. Alice agreed to leave Vétheuil, her melancholy thoughts about her ruined husband, and her earlier life at Rottembourg.

After the open countryside of Vétheuil, Monet found Poissy suburban and unattractive. Early in 1883, when his lease on the house in Poissy was due to expire, he embarked on the hunt for a new home for his substantial household. On April 5, he wrote to Durand-Ruel: "I was planning to get going today to find a house, because we'll have to leave Poissy in ten days' time … if I was settled somewhere permanent, I could at least paint and put a brave face on it … tomorrow and the days after, I'm going to go out until I've found a place and a house that suit me."

The next day, he started house-hunting in the area just outside the Ile de France, the region surrounding Paris. He traveled west toward Normandy on the Le Havre train, following the course of the Seine, and got off at Vernon, intending to explore the small villages of the Seine valley, which had always appealed to him.

Along the local line running from Pacy-sur-Eure to Gisors, Monet discovered Giverny, a village of 279 inhabitants which stretched over a mile or so. The people were farmers and market gardeners, and the names of the streets and lanes seemed to have changed little since the Middle Ages. There were Press Street, Dovecote Street, Candlemaker Street, Streets of the Jews, and Tithe Barn Lane. The main road split into two at the edge of the village, the upper half winding past the local government offices in the *mairie,* past the church, and down a fairly steep slope to rejoin the lower half, also known as King's Road,

GIVERNY. - Maison ancienne

or the chemin du Roy. This skirted the southern side of the village running alongside the Vernon-Gisors rail line and the River Ru, a small branch of the River Epte, itself a tributary of the Seine.

Monet loved everything about the place: the shifting quality of the light, the peaceful waters of the Epte, the soft shadows cast by the poplars, the streams meandering through marshy

Giverny in Monet's time was a village with an almost medieval air, composed of half-timbered farmhouses with tiled roofs, barns, and stables. The inhabitants, who mostly worked on the land, regarded members of the Monet household with a certain degree of suspicion: they were newcomers, and Monet preferred to keep himself to himself. But Alice earned their respect through her frequent attendance at the local church.

meadows bright with wild iris, the cool shade of the tree-lined river banks, and in the distance, huge wheatfields bordered by poppies. Some way away, he spotted a house, half-hidden by the flower-decked branches of fruit trees. It was a modest building and, with its long plain facade rendered in pink, its gray shutters, and slate roof, quite unlike the others in the village. A row of windows along one side faced due south and looked out onto a little orchard, with the river beyond. Though by no means grand, it was a solidly built and well-proportioned *maison bourgeoise*, the house of people with some social standing. It would lend itself to improvements and extensions at a later date.

The owner, Louis-Joseph Singeot, agreed to rent the house, which was described in the lease as being "situated in the locality known as 'le pressoir' [the press]" – a reference to its former use as a cider farm. The entire property was enclosed within a wall and consisted of several buildings in addition to two houses and an orchard. In the main house, there were four rooms on the ground floor and another four on the floor above, two attic rooms, an attic, and a cellar. The west side was flanked by a barn, the east by a woodshed, another small shed, and an outhouse. A smaller house contained several rooms, including a kitchen, a storeroom, and a stable.

While Monet had found what he was looking for, however, his financial position was still precarious. Having arranged to move in at the end of April, on the 29th of that month he was again writing to Durand-Ruel:

"At last I'm setting off for Giverny this morning with some of the children. But we're so short of money that Madame Hoschedé can't come with us and she has to be out of the house by 10 o'clock tomorrow. So may I ask you please to give the bearer of this letter one or two hundred-franc notes, whatever you can manage, and send the same sum to me at Giverny, near Vernon, Eure, because we won't have any money at all when we get there."

While they were waiting for their furniture to arrive, the family stayed at a small inn in the village. Though the process of moving in lasted for a full thirteen days, once they had unpacked, Monet and Alice were quick to organize life in their new home. The six older children were put into a boarding school in Vernon, while the two youngest, Michel and Jean-Pierre, went to the village school. Monet had his studio boat moored nearby and stored his painting equipment in the barn. He then turned his attention to the outside and began planning changes in the garden so that there would be plenty of flowers to enjoy and paint.

By the end of the 1880s, Monet's fortunes had improved considerably.

Having failed to find buyers for his painters in Paris, Durand-Ruel took the courageous step in 1883 of organizing an exhibition in London and then, in April 1886, crossing the Atlantic with around 300 canvases, forty-eight of them by Monet. Though Monet objected strongly to his work being shipped off to "the land of the Yankees," the Americans bought his paintings in big enough quantities to allow him to earn a good living from his art; more importantly, the French public began to follow suit. Soon, however, Monet fell out with "Monsieur Durand," whom he accused of building up a collection of his work and preventing other collectors from buying it. He agreed to show his paintings at Georges Petit's attractive gallery in Paris and at provincial exhibitions elsewhere in France. He also took charge of his own sales, cultivating private patrons and deciding his own prices for his paintings.

By 1889, as their exhibitions multiplied, the Impressionists became the toast of fashionable circles in Paris, Monet's work began to fetch incredible sums for the period. *The Seine at Vétheuil* was sold for 7,900 francs,

*The Hoschedé and Monet families pose for a photograph in the shade of the lime trees on a
summer's day a few years after their move to Giverny. Monet himself is standing on the far left
behind Alice and Jean-Pierre Hoschedé, while Michel Monet sits at Alice's feet. Seated at the far
side of the table, from left to right, are Blanche Hoschedé, Jean Monet (Blanche's future husband),
and Germaine Hoschedé. Behind them stands the elegant figure of Jacques Hoschedé. In the
foreground are Marthe Hoschedé and, to her right, Suzanne Hoschedé, Monet's favorite model.*

The White Turkeys for 12,000 francs. The years of bitter struggle and poverty were over. In 1890 Monet arranged to buy the house for 22,000 francs, payable over four years. Though he made frequent painting trips abroad and to other parts of France, Giverny was to remain his home for the rest of his life.

Monet's increasing fame attracted a number of visitors to Giverny, in particular several American artists who came to stay at the nearby Hotel Baudy. At first, Monet was not at all pleased to see "these wretched Americans," as he called them, living in the village. On one of his painting trips, he wrote to Alice that he was worried that his stepdaughters "might have responded favorably to advances from Americans temporarily staying at Giverny." He was unhappy about the thought of Suzanne falling in love with Theodore Butler, a young man "she had met while he was passing through." But another American painter, Theodore Robinson, one of the few that Monet welcomed to the family circle, provided reassurance about Butler's family background. Suzanne and Theodore Butler were married in the little church in Giverny in 1892, just ten days after Monet married Alice there, to "regularize" their situation in time for the big wedding.

During the forty-three years he lived there, Monet gradually made alterations to his home. The general layout of the main house stayed roughly the same, with the double doors leading from the garden to a small central hall from which interconnecting rooms led one into another on each side. But he extended and modernized the kitchen at one end and added a room at the other by converting the barn into a studio drawing room with a short flight of seven steps connecting it to the house.

When it came to decorating the house, Monet was firmly opposed to conventional decorative schemes and to borrowings from the past. During his formative years, fashionable interiors had become highly cluttered and often rather somber. Walls were hidden behind heavy hangings or wallpaper with large floral or leafy patterns. Curtains were lined, sometimes twice over, and windows obscured by half-curtains and blinds so that the light filtering through

ABOVE: *The two youngest members of the household are dressed like twins in sweaters and thick boots: Michel Monet (on the left) was born in 1878, Jean-Pierre Hoschedé in 1877. Close companions, they enjoyed going on expeditions to find new plants or butterflies, and fishing in the nearby Epte.*
LEFT: *Monet wearing clogs and his characteristic soft felt hat, standing in his garden at the end of the 1880s. The photograph was taken by Theodore Robinson, one of the few American painters living in Giverny who Monet entertained at home.*

them was distinctly subdued. Furniture in general became more massive: chairs and sofas were overstuffed and buttoned, covered in velvet and decorated with fringes. There was a tendency toward historical pastiche: dining rooms in sixteenth-century style made a triumphal appearance in petit-bourgeois circles, and the ornate Louis XVI style staged a glittering comeback.

The arrival of Art Nouveau in the 1890s, with its sinuous lines and its exuberant representations of flowers and leaves, may have heralded a break with the popular historicist styles, but Monet preferred a simpler and more individual way of decorating. He employed no interior decorators but relied instead on craftsmen who used their skills to follow his plans. In keeping with the rural nature of his home, he chose materials that were traditional for the area, such as wall tiles from Rouen and Normandy furniture. But to these he added touches of eastern exoticism: a bamboo hat stand in the épicerie, or a colorful rug on the floor of the studio drawing room.

The walls were painted in clear,

RIGHT: *The main entrance to the house at the head of the Grande Allée. The brilliant green of the doors and shutters is a perfect foil for the pink stucco of the facade.*

OPPOSITE: *The second studio, west of the main house was added in 1897. It now provides office and living space for the staff of the Musée Monet. The large hothouse in front of the studio was given over to the cultivation of orchids.*

THE PALETTE

strong colors to provide an interesting yet unobtrusive background for his large collection of prints and paintings. Some of the larger pieces of furniture were painted in the same shades as the walls and paintwork, and where the windows were curtained, the fabric used was mostly light in color.

Outside, the pink rendering applied by a previous owner, nostalgic for the years he spent in Guadaloupe, grew darker; the shutters and the doors were painted a brilliant Veronese green in place of the former gray. The facade was covered with a Virginia creeper that wound from one window to another, its leaves framing the doors on the ground floor which led on to a new veranda shaded by a hornbeam hedge.

As his paintings became more ambitious in scale, Monet needed bigger spaces to work in. At the end of the 1890s, he had a house on the northwestern side of the garden pulled down so that he could erect on the site a building large enough to hold a second studio as well as a photographer's darkroom and additional living rooms and bedrooms for the children. There was also a new garage, for both Monet and Alice became automobile enthusiasts after the family had acquired a Panhard-Levassor in 1901. Finally, between 1914 and 1916, the painter had a third studio built on the northeastern side of the estate in which to work on his large panels of waterlilies.

The House and Garden

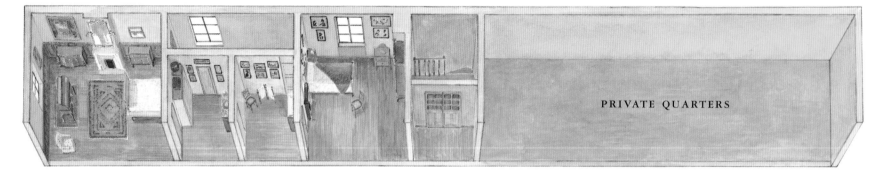

PRIVATE QUARTERS

The second floor, from left to right: Monet's bedroom; Monet's dressing room; Alice's dressing room;
Alice's bedroom; the stairs leading up from the entrance and the laundry room.

The ground floor, from left to right: the studio drawing room; the épicerie; the blue salon;
the entrance; the dining room; the kitchen.

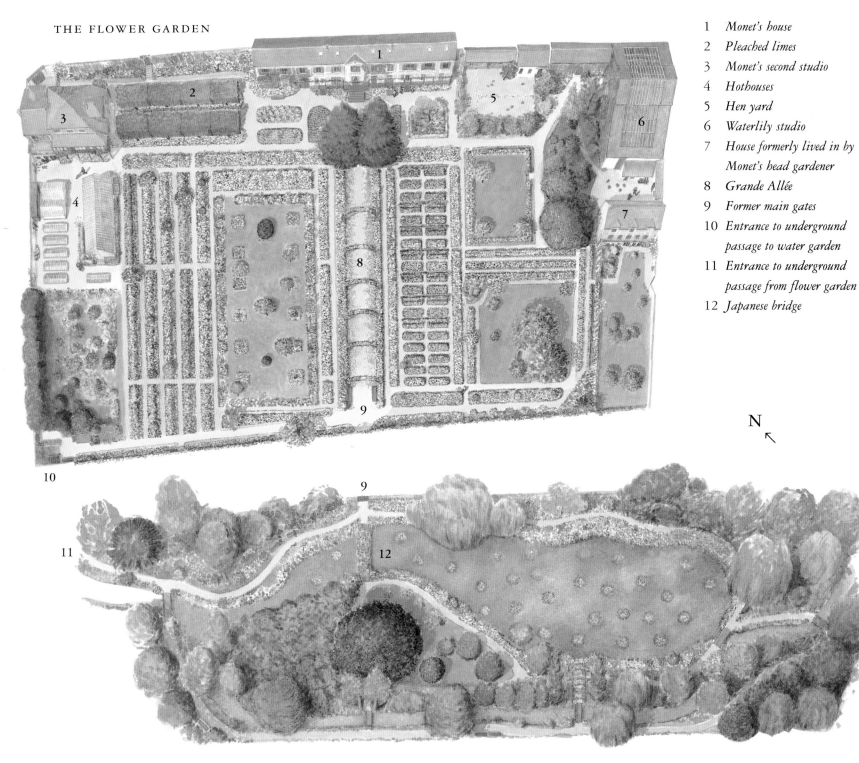

THE FLOWER GARDEN

1 Monet's house
2 Pleached limes
3 Monet's second studio
4 Hothouses
5 Hen yard
6 Waterlily studio
7 House formerly lived in by
   Monet's head gardener
8 Grande Allée
9 Former main gates
10 Entrance to underground
   passage to water garden
11 Entrance to underground
   passage from flower garden
12 Japanese bridge

N

THE WATER GARDEN

The transformation of the neglected orchard and potager into a garden with a dazzling profusion of flowers began almost the minute Monet moved into his new home. Initially, he did the planting and tending himself, with some help from the children, but by 1890 he was wealthy enough to employ six gardeners and to have two greenhouses built. The flower garden ran parallel to the road and was enclosed with nothing more than a low wall and railings, so that any passerby could enjoy its splendors. Writing in 1901, the critic Arsène Alexandre noted "... the garden *is* Monet" and went on to describe the planting:

"If you dig up the carrots and lettuces [in a market garden] and instead plant flowers, but just as close together, you will get wonderful results, providing you are capable of playing on the floral calendar as you would on a piano keyboard, and providing you are an expert with colors. It is this profusion, this sense of flowers crowded together, that gives the garden its whole character ..."

Bright yellows, soft mauves, and reds are used to brilliant effect in the long flowerbeds on the west side of the garden.

In 1893 Monet bought another strip of land beyond the rail line at the end of the flower garden. It bordered the River Ru, a tributary of the Epte, and in 1901 he obtained permission from the municipal authorities to divert the stream so he could enlarge an existing pond to create an extensive water garden. He surrounded it with weeping willows and poplars, rare lilies, azaleas, rhododendrons, and roses, and built a little green Japanese bridge across the pond, around which he would train white and mauve wisterias. Alexandre described "this stretch of water" as "a masterpiece by some goldsmith who has blended together alloys of the most magic metals." Monet spent hours here seated on his bench by the waterlily pond, contemplating the play of light on water, and it inspired his final and most ambitious project, the *Grandes Décorations des Nymphéas*, which he was completing in the months before his death in 1926. The waterlily panels, which were bequeathed to the French nation, remain the most eloquent testimony to Giverny and its creator.

The pond bordered by willows, lilies, hostas, and ferns, looking toward the Japanese bridge.

The
Entrance

Crossing the threshold from the veranda, most visitors would have received their first impression of Monet's unique decorative scheme in this relatively understated entrance at the center of the house. At the heart of a sequence of light-filled rooms on the ground floor, its soft blues formed a counterpoint to the gleaming blue kitchen, the chrome yellows of the dining room, and the vibrant blues of the salon. A modest staircase led up to the second floor girls' bedrooms and the attics where the boys slept. Monet's and Alice's rooms could also be reached this way, or by a more private staircase from the épicerie.

RIGHT: *The hall is the culminating point of the Grande Allée, the path lined with roses and nasturtiums at the height of summer, which is the main north-south axis running through the flower garden. Beyond the green doors in the distance is the water garden, whose Japanese bridge is in exact alignment with the Grande Allée. Furnishings in the hall are confined to an umbrella stand and a mirror. During Monet's day, hats and coats were hung in the épicerie to reduce the clutter.*

LEFT AND RIGHT: *When light filters through the latticework of the doors, it creates an attractive filigree of broken shadows on the pale walls, reminiscent of the play of light on water.*
BELOW: *The hall floor consists of encaustic tiles in the same colors - terra cotta and cream - as those in most of the other downstairs rooms, but here the pattern is formed from small triangles instead of squares or diamonds.*

Monet enjoyed planning tours of the house and grounds for those who came to visit him. He varied the order of viewing according to the time of year and how well he knew his guests, but he usually started from the entrance hall, reserving the route that began with his studio drawing room for those who wanted to see his paintings first of all.

Looking through the hall's double doors, past the uprights of the vine-festooned veranda, visitors would have seen banks of flowerbeds, planted so that there was a continuous succession of colorful blooms from the beginning

of spring to the first frosts of winter. The large mirror in its blue frame hanging on the wall near the door furthered this sense of perspective, reflecting the greenery from the outside and bringing the garden into the house.

The water garden was not visible from here, but its existence was hinted at in the two colors of the walls and woodwork. The walls were painted a green-blue color, mixed according to a secret recipe, to give a slight surface sheen. The doors were painted pastel blue, with the baseboards and moldings picked out in darker blue.

The Dining Room

T his large sunny room facing due south provided an elegant setting in which Monet and Alice, who were great connoisseurs of food and wine, enjoyed dining with family and friends. One of the visitors who best described the convivial atmosphere at Giverny was the art critic Gustave Geffroy. "In that modest house which was nevertheless so sumptuous in its decor," he wrote, "we derived enormous pleasure from sitting around a table where the food was served in generous portions but was always prepared with finesse, and enlivened by light wines of every possible hue."

Decorated at a time when heavy curtains, dark colors, and elaborate trimmings were the fashion, the dining room was painted with unusually bright colors. Monet's bold scheme combined "light chrome yellow, with contrasting ornamental moldings in pure chrome yellow against a gilt background." Lecanu, the local house painters from whose records this description comes, must have been hoping to provide a more elaborate scheme for the artist than this unified finish, but the effect was striking in its simplicity.

The light tone of the walls and ceiling, with moldings, dado, and door frames picked out in brighter yellow, was repeated in the furniture, and the whole was given a final layer of lacquer in a satin finish. The low ceiling, typical of a Normandy farmhouse, was painted white to add a sense of space.

Diners were seated at the large table on wooden chairs painted in two tones of yellow to match the walls and cornices. With their rush seats and decorative backs suggestive of sheaves of bulrushes or wheat, they were a typical early nineteenth-century Normandy design, yet one that was

LEFT: The dining room as visitors would have seen it when entering from the hall. The brilliance of the yellow is intensified when viewed against the blues of the hall and kitchen on each side.
BELOW: The simple terra-cotta and cream colored tiles used in most rooms on the ground floor are here laid in a diagonal pattern. Rush matting is placed under the dining table.

fashionable in avant-garde circles: William Morris based his Rossetti chair of 1865 on this traditional French pattern.

A pair of matching Normandy cabinets, also painted yellow, was ranged along one wall. These held the family collection of blue and white china, its color scheme echoed in the Rouen tiles of the mantelpiece. The French doors leading to the veranda were hung with unobtrusive, soft cream curtains to let the maximum amount of sunlight flood in. At night, the room was lit by two simple yellow opaline lamps suspended from the ceiling.

Once the room had acquired the appearance of a unified whole, the walls became a backcloth on which Monet could hang paintings. Initially, he chose family portraits for the dining room, but these were later replaced by Japanese prints in plain black frames.

Further touches of color were provided by the pots on the mantelpiece, glazed in shades of green. Most of them came from the area around Nîmes in the south of France, and they were all plain, except for the tall vase in the center, decorated with motifs resembling bats.

The Japanese prints in the dining room are still hung as they were in Monet's day. His personal collection consisted of 231 prints, over half of which were works by Utamaro, Hokusai, and Hiroshige. Dating mostly from the eighteenth and nineteenth centuries, they cover a wide variety of subject matter, from local flora and fauna to portraits of courtesans.

According to Octave Mirbeau, Monet first came across Japanese prints while he was staying in Holland in 1871. Having been to a grocer's shop, he returned home to find that his purchases were wrapped in special paper printed with images of great beauty, delicately depicting scenes of everyday life in Japan. Surprised and intrigued by this discovery, he went back the following day to acquire the whole pile of prints which the shopkeeper was using for packaging. Later, Monet claimed to have bought his first print in Le Havre in 1856, when he was sixteen years old, though this is open to question.

What fascinated him was the skillful way that Japanese artists reproduced their world through a combination of color and line. Some even depicted the same scene several times under different light conditions (an idea which Monet

Shichiri-ga-hama in the Province of Sagami, undated, Hokusai

Mountains and Rivers on the Kiso Road, undated, attributed to Hiroshige

took up in his series paintings of Haystacks, Wheatstacks, and Poplars).

Of the collectors and dealers who brought Japanese art to a wider public, the most important were Tadamasa Hayashi, a frequent guest at Giverny, and Samuel Bing, whose store in Paris was often visited by the painter. Hayashi alone imported more than 150,000 prints from Japan and, in his turn, began to collect the works of French artists, including Monet. In 1893 he organized the first exhibition of Impressionist paintings in Japan.

Young Woman with Her Face Reflected in a Mirror, c.1791, Utamaro

The Flight of Butterflies, c.1799, Utamaro

The Island of Tsukuda and the District of Fukagawa under a Full Moon, undated, Hiroshige

Crane Perched on a Pine at Sunrise,
undated, Hiroshige

The Island of Tsukuda and the District of Fukagawa, undated, Hiroshige

Amadai and Mouo, undated, Hiroshige

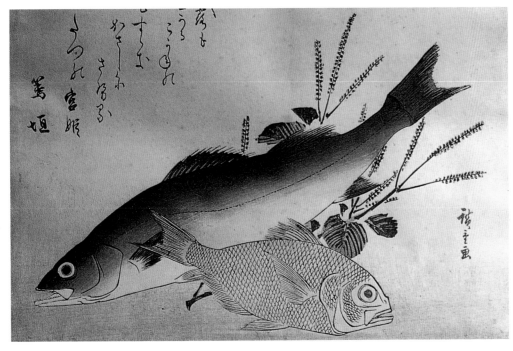

Suzuki, Lateolabrax Japonicus, and Kinmedai Lying on a branch of Shiso, undated, Hiroshige

Crane and Young Perched on a Pine at Sunrise, 1854, Hiroshige

Meals in the Monet household were timed to the minute. Since Monet did much of his painting from life in the open air, every moment of daylight was precious to him, and he had his breakfast soon after dawn, usually alone but sometimes accompanied by Blanche, herself a painter. He would eat roasted meat, broiled chitterling sausages, some Stilton (the most Gallic of British cheeses), French bread, and Normandy butter with marmalade, accompanied by both china tea and a glass of milk. Lunch followed punctually at 11.30 A.M. and dinner at 7 P.M. A gong was struck twice to summon everybody, and lateness was not tolerated.

During their early days together, Alice had to struggle to make ends meet, and any entertaining was necessarily on a modest scale. But her concern was always to make sure that all her guests felt at home and Geffroy paid specific tribute in his biography of Monet to the warmth of her welcome.

Whether guests were present or not, the menu was remarkably varied. Monet liked the country dishes that form the substantial repertoire of French classical cuisine. As his fortunes improved, he bought additional land in the village to create a kitchen garden, so the family

was able to eat food grown on his own estate. He also bred and kept hens and ducks in the henyard on one side of the house, so his own poultry could be offered to family and guests.

Lunch and dinner usually consisted of at least three courses, including a salad, but desserts in the evening tended to be less elaborate affairs than those made for lunch. Paul, the butler, served the dishes in rapid succession since Monet did not like too long a pause between courses. But the artist preferred to toss the salad and to carve meat and game himself at the table.

As an early riser, Monet hated going to bed late and preferred to entertain guests at lunchtime. So insistent was he on eating at 11.30 A.M. precisely that he would advise visitors to forget their passion for cars and travel by train so that they could be sure of arriving on time at the nearby town of Vernon, where he would send his chauffeur to pick them up. Other visitors arrived by water. The painter and naval architect Gustave Caillebotte and the dramatist Octave Mirbeau, who both lived nearby and were keen gardeners as well as close friends, often came to lunch by boat along the Seine.

Initially, the luncheon guests were

the painters Monet described as "the companions of my youth": Camille Pissarro, Alfred Sisley, Auguste Renoir, Johann-Barthold Jongkind, and Eugène Boudin. As he grew more successful, his circle of visitors expanded to include painters such as Edgar Degas and Berthe Morisot, writers such as Stéphane Mallarmé, Anatole France, and Paul Valéry, the politician Georges Clemenceau, and patrons from the United States and Japan. At one time, Monet even played host to the members of the prestigious Académie Goncourt, whose lunches he regularly attended.

Mealtime conversation at Monet's table was lively. Stimulated by good food and interesting company, visitors enjoyed the opportunity to compare their work and plan future journeys. From time to time, however, the convivial atmosphere was disrupted by strange behavior on the part of the guests. In July 1889, for example, the sculptor Auguste Rodin came to lunch, and both Mirbeau and one of the Goncourt brothers reported that this "satyr," as they called him, spent the entire time eyeing the Hoschedé girls in such a way that each of them in turn had to get up from the table and leave the room. On another occasion, in

November 1895, Monet invited Rodin, Mirbeau, Geffroy, and Clemenceau to lunch to meet the comparatively unknown Paul Cézanne, whose table manners were somewhat rough and ready: he would habitually scrape his soup plate and eat from his knife or use his fingers. So overcome was Cézanne

Monet photographed in the dining room by Nadar at the turn of the century. A demanding gourmet, the artist prided himself on the excellence of his hospitality. Lunch was offered to favored visitors, who were also invited to stroll around the garden and inspect past and present work in the studios.

when Rodin shook hands with him that he knelt at his feet in gratitude. None of this odd behavior bothered Monet, who always remained loyal to his friends.

If he was not entertaining, Monet would return to his easel after coffee and liqueurs had been served in the studio drawing room.

RIGHT: *The two glass-fronted cabinets that house the everyday china are typical early nineteenth-century pieces from the Caux region of Normandy. The cornices are surmounted by basket-handle arches with double scrolls.*

OPPOSITE: *When important guests were expected, Alice preferred to bring out a white porcelain set of dishes with wide yellow rims and a border of blue. Monet's improved financial circumstances had allowed him to commission this set from the Cristallerie Royale de Champagne, to be made according to his own design.*

Monet believed that a beautiful dinner service was one of the keys to a successful meal, and the twin cabinets at Giverny housed china as elegant as the meals served there. The color scheme was a subtle blend of blues and whites from the finest manufacturers in Europe. The Creil faience used for everyday meals, with its delicate Japanese-inspired decoration of cherry blossom and little fans, fitted in wonderfully well with the odd pieces of Meissen and Sèvres ware in hard-paste porcelain, so white and smooth it had a bluish tinge.

Since lunches and dinners invariably began with a hot hors d'oeuvre, followed by a meat or fish dish, and sometimes both, an enormous selection of china was called for. Among the many Creil dinner plates, soup plates, side plates, dessert dishes, and cake plates, there were a few examples of Dresden, Rouen, and Nevers china, the idea being to achieve a happy marriage between faience, porcelain, and bone china. There was also a huge variety of serving dishes: soup tureens and vegetable dishes, coffeepots and pitchers for hot chocolate, salad bowls, and many other pieces of every imaginable size and shape.

A large table was needed in the dining room. Even for everyday family meals, there would be ten places laid for Monet, Alice, her six children, and his two. A special system of leaves hidden beneath the tablecloth allowed the table to be extended so that up to sixteen people could be seated on special occasions. To show off the china to best advantage, the table cloth was always solid yellow and usually entirely smooth, since in those days people took the trouble to roll cloths instead of folding them. The flatware was of fine silver, and every setting was given a different stemless glass for each wine to be drunk at the meal. Only clear glass was used, since Monet thought that colored glass made the wine appear unappetizing. Table decorations were confined to a few small glass dishes simply arranged with fresh flowers from the garden or greenhouse.

Crystal wine decanters stood on one of the sideboards (left). Monet preferred white wines, especially Sancerre, but on special occasions when great vintages were served, they would be decanted from their bottles to breathe. Lunches often ended with fruit (above). The usual custom was then to retire to the studio drawing room for coffee, accompanied by small squares of fruit jellies (right) flavored with local raspberries, blackcurrants, and bilberries, and a glass of homemade plum brandy.

The Kitchen and Cellar

Adjoining the yellow dining room, the spacious blue-tiled kitchen had a glass-paneled door and two uncurtained windows opening onto the veranda, so the cook could enjoy views of the garden framed by trees, and step outside to where hens and ducks roamed through the nearby farmyard. A separate door led down to the cellar, where fruit and wine were stored along with the gardening tools. Monet himself rarely set foot in his kitchen, but as a demanding gourmet, he took an intense interest in everything that happened there. During his time at Giverny, the kitchen underwent several alterations and modernizations in response to the changing needs of his household.

The kitchen was decorated in shades of pale blue, with detailing delineated in darker blue. Glossy paintwork and the blue and white Rouen tiles covering the walls formed sparkling surfaces that were easy to clean; the tiles above the stove are a more recent addition. The large cooking range, rustic wooden furniture, and the simple hexagonal terra-cotta floor tiles often found in Normandy houses combined to create an impression of simplicity.

Every piece of equipment had its appointed place. Cleaning products were lined up under the sink. In addition to the floor wax and furniture polish, there were natural sponges, bars of glycerine soap, scouring powder, insecticide, and metal polish. A cupboard housed brooms, feather dusters, and bundles of wool for polishing the wooden floors. Also stored here were cotton aprons, cotton floor cloths, and a canvas bag full of clothes pins.

Alice's zeal as a housekeeper sometimes caused Monet concern. In 1884, while away in Italy, he wrote to her: "I'm worried that you're taking your love of your home too far, and that you'll wear yourself out with all your scouring and polishing."

RIGHT AND OPPOSITE:
The focal point of the kitchen was the large cooking range. Fueled by wood or coal, it was placed between the window and fireplace so that fumes could be directed out of the room. It had hot plates whose temperature could be adjusted, a plate warmer, and two ovens, so the cook and her helpers could prepare sauces, meat, or fish dishes, steam vegetables, and bake cakes all at the same time.
OVERLEAF: *Above the stove, a shelf bordered with blue and white tiles was crammed with an array of utensils: stoneware bottles, earthenware pitchers, small dishes for baking pâtés and terrines, matchboxes, thin string, and a pestle and mortar for crushing salt.*

THE PALETTE

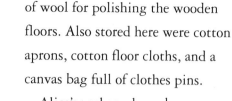

During Monet's forty-three years at Giverny, a number of cooks came to work for the family at different times, but there was no doubt that Marguerite was his favorite. She was married to Paul, who acted as butler and odd-job man. With one or two kitchen maids to help her, she worked for the most part in silence, believing that if a dish was well cooked there was no need to discuss it. She had to work at a frantic pace to have everything ready on time, because Monet insisted on the highest standards and absolute punctuality. And since the kitchen was right next to the dining room, there could be no clattering of pots and pans during meals.

The menus for the week were planned by Alice and frequently put Marguerite's talents to the test, especially if guests were expected.

There were also family celebrations to cater for. When Alice's daughter Germaine was married, for example,

There were always cakes and pastries to be made, for there were many sweet-toothed members of the family. A special table was set aside for making pastry; favorite desserts were apple popovers and tarts filled with plums from the garden, which were browned in the oven.

the guests sat down to a six-course lunch, which included turbot with Hollandaise sauce, shrimp, roast venison, turkey, and sherbet. The family photograph album contains evidence of many similar celebrations. The artist had come a long way since the time when he had to endure fasts dictated by necessity, relieved only by the bread rolls that Renoir had brought him from his mother's table.

Monet's painting expeditions took him all over France, as well as to England and Scandinavia, and he usually returned from his travels with new ideas for the cook based on food he had eaten during his travels. The Giverny notebooks show that fellow artists and other friends, knowing Monet's love of food, contributed their own recipes as well. The artist was particularly fond of the strong-flavored herbs that feature in Mediterranean cuisine. He also retained a love for the seafood he had eaten during his

Monet was very fond of red cabbage cooked with Reine de Reinette apples from the orchard, vinegar, gray shallots, and mild onions stuck with cloves and seasoned with nutmeg. It was the perfect accompaniment for the game birds that Alice's sons supplied during the hunting season.

childhood in the Norman port of Le Havre, and for the other traditional dishes of Normandy. When he was away, he sometimes despatched packages of local delicacies to the family at home. In one of his letters to Alice from the port of Etretat, he wrote: "... I shall probably send you for Wednesday a batch of crabs and some tiny lobsters. They're quite delicious at the moment, and I'm sure the children will enjoy them. I'll put some shrimp in for you too ..." On another occasion he sent tangerines from the Riviera.

LEFT: *Monet's deluxe range was manufactured around the turn of the century by the firm of Briffault. The body was made of thick sheet steel, while the door edges and decorative flourishes consisted of polished steel. In addition to cooking, the range heated the water in a built-in tank, while a special type of faucet with a press screw allowed the water to be run off without any danger of flooding.*

RIGHT: *With so many meals to prepare, the kitchen remained a hive of activity throughout the day. Not only did Monet's cook require a large amount of equipment, she also had to make sure that implements for every conceivable culinary job were kept within reach. There were saucepans and skillets, fish kettles and sauté pans, pancake griddles and stockpots, all kept scoured and gleaming. A large tinned-copper preserving pan was used to make the jams and jellies that saw the household through the winter.*

In the absence of refrigeration, salt was needed in large quantities. It was used not only for seasoning, but for preserving pork and other meats. Sea salt from Guérande was kept in the seat of a special chair, and the large crystals were crushed with a pestle and mortar before being added to food.

If turbot was on the menu, it would be cooked in time-honored fashion in a special fish kettle called a turbotière, just covered by a very light court-bouillon. There was no question of masking the natural taste of the produce by using spices, so the cooking liquid was merely flavored with a few slices of lemon, three or four bay leaves, a little bunch of parsley, a few peppercorns, and a handful of sea salt, so the fish could retain all its marine flavor. Hollandaise sauce made in a bain-marie was the usual accompaniment. Shrimp would be mixed with garlic and parsley, and sautéed over a fierce heat.

For the most part, the emphasis was on local produce. Turkeys and chickens came from Monet's own poultry runs, ducks from the pond, game and fish from the neighboring countryside. After he had acquired the additional piece of land in the rue du Chêne at the other end of the village in 1890, Monet was able to cultivate his own herbs, vegetables, and soft fruit. Florimond presided over this kitchen garden, where the beds were laid out with geometrical precision. Once it was established, Monet visited it every day to make a personal selection of fruit and vegetables. The delicious young peas and carrots, the leeks and potatoes for the soup, the sprigs of parsley and tarragon, the lettuce leaves and strawberries he had chosen were then picked in the early hours of the following morning to be conveyed to the kitchen in a large basket.

Monet prided himself on being able to serve food grown on his own land, whether it was vegetables and herbs (left) or soft fruit like plums (far left). This fresh produce was supplemented with delicacies from the local woods, such as fleshy ceps and golden chanterelles. Vegetables were washed in the flat stone sink and were often steamed, as Monet particularly favored this method of cooking.

Normandy is the apple orchard of France, renowned for its cider and the
apple brandy Calvados. When Monet first moved to Giverny, his house
was known as the Maison du Pressoir, after the cider presses of the
neighborhood, and cider was probably once made in the cellar. The garden
still boasts a range of fruit trees, particularly apples and pears. A number
of varieties of apple were grown for different purposes, some for making
cider, some for eating, some for cooking. The versatile pippin types, such as
Reine de Reinette and Belle de Boskoop, were an important ingredient
in both sweet and savory local dishes.

Leading directly off the kitchen, the cool dry basement area, with its floor of beaten earth, served as a wine cellar and a storehouse for fruit and gardening equipment.

Monet's taste in wine was wide-ranging, as his account books show, and he ordered wine from Burgundy, Bordeaux, and the Loire to be kept in his cellars, alongside barrels of cider and homemade fruit brandy. Sylvain, who also helped with the cars, was responsible for looking after the wine. Working by the light of a small portable lamp, he would broach a barrel, insert a spigot, and carefully draw off a few drops to test the alcohol content, before tasting the vintage.

Although there is no record of whether Monet was a connoisseur of champagne, he did like to serve it on festive occasions, or when he and Alice were able to relax alone together. A letter he wrote to Alice from Bordighera in Italy on March 21, 1884, makes this clear: "... I want to put in an order for two bottles of good champagne and some morel mushrooms – that's what I fancy for some reason; and I shall smoke a pipe of good tobacco on the studio divan! I'm really looking forward to it!"

LEFT: *The cellar had built-in shelves to hold preserving jars full of fruit, plums and apricots bottled in syrup for the winter, and cherries steeped in brandy. Pears and apples were stored in slatted racks with enough space between them to prevent rot from spreading.*

ABOVE AND RIGHT: *Sylvain used a large selection of equipment to bottle the wine. There were pewter and copper funnels, unused corks and corkscrews, a special glass for assessing taste and bouquet, and spigots waiting to be inserted into unbroached vats.*

The Blue Salon

Situated between the main entrance hall and the épicerie, this essentially feminine room was the setting for family activities. Here Monet, Alice, and the children gathered to read and sew, play card games, or listen to music. One lunch visitor, struck by the intimacy of its atmosphere, wrote: "Once the meal was over, we returned to the studio to drink our coffee, via the blue salon, where Monet has his library. That was where we saw Madame Monet, surrounded by her children and Monet's – a dazzling glimpse of a woman calmly happy in the bosom of the family, her bright eyes shining beneath a halo of powdered hair."

Before moving to Giverny, Monet wrote to Paul Durand-Ruel in mid-April 1883 of his delight in the house he had found there, which offered "the tranquility that is the first requirement if one is to work well." That peace is very much in evidence in this calm room, where the pale blue walls form a harmonious background for some of the painter's collection of Japanese prints, including two scenes of women fishing by Chikanobu and Kunisada, and a series of landscapes by Hiroshige, Kuniyoshi, and Yoshitora. As in the dining room, a deeper version of the color used on the walls highlights the moldings. Monet was in the habit of changing the color he used here: at different times the room was also painted in a similar manner in shades of mauve.

THE PALETTE

The blue salon is lit only by a single set of french doors opening out onto the veranda, but its light colors make it appear bright and airy. The floor tiles are more ornate than those in the other downstairs rooms, with their stylized white flowers and curves outlined against a tan background.

For the painter himself, this intimate room was primarily a library, where he kept his large collection of books on botany. Among these were the twenty-three volume *La Flore des jardins d'Europe* (A European Flora), a gardening dictionary, books on the cultivation of orchids, and his copies of the *Revue horticulturelle*, a French horticultural journal to which he subscribed for more than thirty years between 1893 and 1925. But his

LEFT: *Identical in design to the cabinets holding glass and china in the dining room, this traditional piece from the Caux region of Normandy is painted the same colors as the walls. Monet kept some of his many volumes on gardening behind its glass doors.*
RIGHT: *As the two doors leading into the blue salon are not directly opposite each other, the sense of the long sweep of rooms on the ground floor is maintained by this strategically placed mirror.*

"I've just been reading Flaubert's letters. A wonderfully interesting book, and what a wonderful stylist." He also admired the work of Edgar Allan Poe and the eighteenth-century essayist Saint-Simon.

Monet's was a music-loving household. Marthe, the eldest of the Hoschedé girls, played the piano, and the painter himself would sometimes sing a few songs in his fine, clear voice. An early type of phonograph, which used cylinders instead of records, allowed the Monets to listen to music at home.

Since the family was such a large one and the room relatively small, much of the furniture was lightweight and easy to move to suit different purposes. A small couch ranged along one wall was covered in an attractive silk with a Japanese-style pattern. Folding tables of the kind used on board ships provided movable surfaces on which the children and, later, the grandchildren could play cards or set out a board game. There were low wooden upright chairs with rush seats and a charming miniature bentwood Thonet chair, just the right size for Alice's granddaughters to play a game with their dolls.

library was not exclusively devoted to gardening; the bookshelves also held volumes on art and esthetics. Monet, Alice, and the children gathered here to read and sew, to play games and listen to music. When Monet was feeling relaxed, he would read aloud to the family; the painter Delacroix's *Journal* was a particular favorite. Monet's circle of friends and acquaintances included many men of letters, such as Octave Mirbeau, the poet Stéphane Mallarmé, and the novelist Guy de Maupassant. He was also a passionate admirer of Flaubert, once writing to his friend Gustave Caillebotte:

ABOVE: *Once Monet had built his second studio in the garden and no longer used the studio drawing room as a place of work, the family could make as much noise as they liked without fear of disturbing him. Music was listened to on the phonograph, although the sound that issued from the large trumpet would have been rather crude.*

OPPOSITE: *Other pastimes that took place in the blue drawing room included embroidery. Alice was an accomplished seamstress and enjoyed sewing while she talked to her daughters or watched over the games of her grandchildren. The family also loved card games, during which liqueurs might be served in the Murano glasses that Monet and Alice brought back with them from their trip to Venice.*

The Epicerie

V

As its name suggests, this room was mainly a store for flavorings and exotic spices, as well as for other dry goods and table linen. It also served as a cloakroom or foyer, where coats and hats could be left. The épicerie had a door to the outside, allowing Monet to conduct art dealers or journalists straight from the garden to the studio without passing through the family rooms. Visitors could also be taken up the private staircase leading to Monet's bedroom, where works by his contemporaries hung. Those who had been invited to lunch would follow a more intimate route through the épicerie and blue salon to the dining room.

The decoration was simple. Silky green walls, with woodwork painted in lavender gray and powder blue, formed a muted background for the tall hat stand and for a wooden sideboard, two traditional egg boxes, and a selection of Japanese prints. Terra-cotta and white floor tiles were laid in a diamond pattern.

Despite the unassuming size and the essentially functional nature of the room, the furnishings reflected many of the preoccupations of Monet's household. A love of the outdoor life was evident in the hats that festooned the bamboo stand with its central mirror. Hard-wearing straw from Bangkok, a flexible Panama, and some English cloth caps were kept here alongside the soft small-brimmed felt hat which appears in so many of the photographs of Monet at work in his garden. A few silk umbrellas stood ready to offer shelter from the Normandy showers, alongside the cream-colored parasols used in sunnier weather by Alice and her daughters. Nearby was a butterfly box, where the boys stored the specimens they collected during expeditions along the valley and then pressed between sheets of blotting paper.

LEFT: *The sateen parasols lined with green that were kept in the épicerie found their way into some of Monet's paintings, including* Woman with Parasol Facing Right, *painted in 1886. Alice's eighteen-year-old daughter Suzanne posed on the banks of Nettle Island for this picture; Monet was clearly fascinated by the green shadow the parasol cast on her white dress.* RIGHT: *Hats for all weathers were hung on the bamboo hat stand above the umbrellas.*

THE PALETTE

Also stored here was the table linen; pure linen tablecloths from the Vosges; fringed napkins and honeycomb traycloths, hemmed by hand; and a few remnants of muslin and sturdy cotton ready to make a new apron, or coverall.

First and foremost, however, the épicerie was a testimony to the whole family's sophisticated delight in good food. While Monet's standards were high, the compiling of the week's menus and the organization of regular supplies were left to Alice. The menu called for a variety of exotic ingredients – cloves, saffron, nutmeg, and juniper – in addition to the staples available locally. Since they needed to be kept at a constant temperature, they were stored here, away from the variable heat of the kitchen. From time to time, Alice would accompany Monet on his trips to Paris "to savor the delights of art and good eating" and to replenish her stocks from the high-class grocers of the capital. In between lunches at Prunier's or supper at the equally famous Drouant near the Opéra, they would visit the counter of the Compagnie Coloniale at Hédiard in the Place de la Madeleine, which furnished red and yellow caddies of

Lapsang Souchong tea. Candy flavored with honey or mint and chocolates for the children were bought from Fouquet. A few particularly tempting items would be locked away, including the oriental bonbons known as "Bosphore" and the Petit Beurre cookies known as "Caifa". But some of the imported delicacies were kept on top of the sideboard, together with a colorful array of containers for other foodstuffs.

RIGHT: *Standing beneath Yoshitoshi's* Battle for Odai Castle *and two* Waterfalls *by Hokusai, the sideboard contained an anthology of tastes from around the world in the form of berries, peels, powders, and roots. On the top stood earthenware pitchers; tall stoneware jars full of intensely flavored olive oil from Provence; glass bottles containing bronze-colored ceps, golden chanterelle mushrooms, preserved fruit and vegetables. There was also the invaluable coulis of fruit from the garden, which brought the scents and flavors of summer to winter meals.*
LEFT: *On the walls hung two shallow wooden cabinets. These were originally designed to hold eggs, although their function was mainly decorative since the eggs were actually stored in the cellar. One had a latticework door, echoing Japanese designs, while the blue and white panel of the other was reminiscent of Dutch ceramics.*

Monet's fascination with the
Far East could be seen not only
in the look of the hat stand and
the suggestion of bamboo in the
moldings on the sideboard, but
in the Japanese prints adorning
the walls of the épicerie and the
staircase leading up to his
bedroom. The prints covered a
number of different themes
explored in his painting, echoing
his love of nature. The four
Hiroshige prints in one frame on
the left-hand wall at the foot of
the stairs show different
Japanese landscapes.

A Carp, undated, Hiroshige

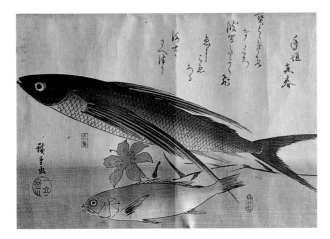

A Flying Fish, undated, Hiroshige

The Salon in a Foreign Merchant's House in Yokohama,
undated, Sadahide (right).
*Monet owned a number of prints by Sadahide showing
European and American merchants in Yokohama. Following
centuries of isolation from the rest of the world, the Japanese
port was opened to foreigners in 1859. Sadahide's series,
which was completed two years later, documents his
fascination with the new clothes and customs the strangers
brought with them.*

VI

The Studio Drawing Room

One of the first alterations Monet made to the house was to convert the high-ceilinged outbuilding adjoining one side into a room that would double as a studio and drawing room. He had stored his canvases and equipment there since he arrived, but now wooden flooring was laid over the bare earth, and large windows cut into the walls to give views of the garden and the main entrance. With plenty of wall space to hang his paintings and a selection of comfortable seating, the barn was transformed into a place for working and entertaining.

When Monet arrived at Giverny, he brought with him the floating studio made from a rowing boat in which he had painted during his years at Argenteuil and Vétheuil, and for which he now had a special boathouse made on the Ile aux Orties (Nettle Island), a small island in the Seine. He claimed he had never seen the need for a conventional artist's *atelier*. In 1880 he commented to the journalist Emile Taboureux, "I don't understand how people can shut themselves in a room. To draw, yes; to paint, no." And though the new room at the Maison du Pressoir was designed very much as a working area with its large windows, he made sure that it was also used as a living room. Alice and the children could read here; friends would come for after-lunch conversation and important guests to view his paintings. On Geffroy's first visit to the house in 1886, he saw a room full of life and youthfulness, where "girls, young people, adolescents, the children and stepchildren of Monet [were] united

around him and Mme Monet."

The painter spent as much time as possible in the open air with his easel and paints, remaining outdoors, as the critic Georges Jeanniot put it, "in any sort of weather." But the studio drawing room provided a refuge in which to take stock of his progress. "This is where Monet brings the work he's done during the day," wrote Geffroy, "and then contemplates it for hours at a time, contemplating it as I used to see him doing with his canvases at Belle-Ile, cleaning it, adding the finishing touches, harmonizing it."

Indeed, many of Monet's important works were completed here, including the landscape studies he brought back from his travels to the French coast between 1884 and 1889. The series of Haystacks, Wheatstacks, and Poplars of the early 1890s were all based on subjects he found within a short walk of the house. Though their progressions of shadow and color were clearly charted on the spot, the finishing touches were added in the studio.

Poppy Field (Giverny), *1891. The countryside around Giverny furnished Monet with subjects for many compositions; this picture was painted in a field near Essarts, and the Giverny hill is visible in the background. The proximity of his motifs made it easy for Monet to set off for a day's painting with his wheelbarrow full of blank canvases. Blanche often accompanied him.*

ABOVE: *The studio drawing room as it looked in 1913, when the journalist André Arnyvelde visited Monet and photographed him for an article he was writing. The artist stands in the middle of the room holding the inevitable Caporal rose cigarette. To the right of the window is one of the waterlily paintings he completed before he tackled the theme on a far grander scale in the* Grandes Décorations. *After the complex containing his second studio had been built in 1899 and Monet had moved his easels and brushes there, the studio drawing room became a gallery for Monet's past work. For many visitors, it was as much a source of interest as the celebrated gardens. Hung, in many cases unframed,*
on the pale walls, some of the canvases were simply works for which he had not been able to find a buyer. Others had become so dear to the artist that he could not bear to part with them. As his wealth increased, he was also able to buy back the pictures which he had given to his creditors instead of cash payments in leaner years.

OPPOSITE: *In addition to the wide variety of seating, Monet also kept two desks here. He was a prolific correspondent and left over 2,000 letters on his death. Apart from the more intimate messages he sent Alice almost every day when he was away, he maintained contact with a wide circle of writers and painters, including Mallarmé, Boudin, Renoir, and Sisley.*

ABOVE: *The furnishings of the studio drawing room were an informal mixture of lightweight wicker chairs and tables, which could easily be moved outside, and more traditional and precious pieces.*
OPPOSITE: *Behind Paulin's bronze bust of the painter hung a small ornate Louis XVI mirrored sconce, its two gilded bronze candle-holders emerging from a ram's head. Family photographs jostled for space with finely glazed ceramic pots filled with vibrant flowers from the garden and with the latest artistic journals sent from Paris. It was here, too, that Monet joined Alice's son Jean-Pierre, a keen botanist, in compiling a herbarium of dried petals and unusual plants for future study.*

Seven wooden steps led down to the studio from the épicerie. After the comparatively small rooms of the house, the studio drawing room seemed very large. Indeed, Monet had a pitch pine screen with a glass panel specially made so that he could divide the space temporarily in two. This gave him a separate area in which to study his notebooks and consult botanical reference works before sketching out new planting schemes for his flowerbeds or drafting plans for the garden at one of his two desks.

The furniture was an attractive jumble of pieces in different styles,

some modern and some traditional. It was ranged around the perimeter of the room so as to leave an empty space in the middle from which to view the rows of canvases which the painter hung edge to edge on the walls. The unusual height of the ceiling meant that the pictures could be displayed in tiers and tilted slightly to make them easily visible from below.

Not all the works of art on display here were by Monet himself. An imposing bust of the artist by Paulin stood on a chest. There was a marble sculpture of a woman and child by Rodin and a medallion of a little girl carved by Renoir. For it was here that the painter kept his mementoes, from the tokens of friendship he had received from fellow artists to the yellowing photographs tucked informally into the frame of a mirror.

An upholstered daybed, cushioned couches, and a collection of rattan and wicker chairs created a relaxing environment. A large table and a number of shelves provided surfaces on which to put books, family snapshots, and other small treasures. Plain curtains hung at the large windows, and kilims relieved the potentially gloomy effect of the dark wood floor.

LEFT: *While the painter was working in his studio, he would not be disturbed. At other times, however, the room became a setting for family activities. Both Monet and Alice were keen on reading, and in the winter, when there were not so many visitors, they enjoyed the works of Tolstoy and Ibsen as well as the novels of French writers like Balzac and Flaubert. When Blanche took over Alice's role as companion and housekeeper after her mother's death, she would often relax here after dinner over a game of backgammon with her stepfather.*

ABOVE: *The studio drawing room led directly from the épicerie, as this early photograph shows. The creation of the interior door, the installation of the short flight of stairs, and the provision of wooden floorboards were among the first improvements to be made to the house.*

By the end of the century, Monet's earnings were considerable (in 1899, for example, he made over quarter of a million francs from the sale of paintings alone), and he could afford to have a second purpose-built studio with a skylight constructed in the garden. Nevertheless, the studio drawing room continued to be a place in which he kept his favorite work, a representative selection from the different phases of his career. He would generally retire here to enjoy a quiet coffee and liqueur after lunch in front of the open door, before resuming work. It was here, too, that Monet liked to offer coffee and home-made fruit brandy to his guests. As his fame spread, so did the number of people coming to see him, from wealthy patrons and gallery owners to admirers from abroad.

LEFT: *To accompany the drinks, there were cheese straws and honey bonbons flavored with bergamot and violets.*
RIGHT: *Through what had once been the barn door, Monet could contemplate the wonders of his garden.*

VII

The Waterlily Studio

In stark contrast to the studio drawing room, Monet's third studio at Giverny was a twentieth-century construction of iron trusses, concrete, and glass. It was built, as the painter put it, in order at last "to judge what I have done," for he had already begun work on the large-scale decorative panels which were to be the culmination of his career. Two couches were placed back to back in the center, so that Monet and his guests could view his work in comfort. Otherwise, the only furnishings were some occasional chairs, easels, and the tables on which he kept his equipment.

By the time France entered World War I in August 1914, Monet's life at Giverny had already changed irrevocably. The death of Alice from leukemia in 1911 left him grief-stricken, and he was virtually unable to paint for months. In the following years, his failing eyesight was diagnosed as cataracts. Though not yet severe enough to be removed, they gave him increasing problems with distinguishing color over the next decade. Then, six months before hostilities began, his older son Jean died. Now in his seventy-fifth year, Monet might well have rested on his laurels and given up painting.

Yet it was at this point that he decided to embark upon his most ambitious project – the *Grandes Décorations des Nymphéas* – showing the beauties of his water garden. The subject itself was not new: Monet had begun painting the pond soon after its construction in 1893 and had already produced two entire series, the first of which he exhibited at Durand-Ruel's at the end of 1900 and the second in 1909. But the vast scale of the new pictures was an innovation. Monet had already been experimenting with different formats – upright, square,

and circular – but he now chose to concentrate on canvases about six feet high and up to 20 feet wide. They could be set side by side to create a continuous watery panorama. Monet's ultimate intention was that they should form the sole decoration of an oval or circular room.

Although he had been painting large canvases both outdoors in the garden and in his second studio, there was nowhere he could sit and ponder his work in progress once it had attained such wide dimensions. Initial designs for a new studio in the north-eastern corner of his property were drawn up in 1914, and once the foundations had been laid in August 1915 the construction progressed quickly. Monet was able to start moving in his canvases that fall, although the official opening took place the following year. The occasion was marked by a special lunch given to selected members of the Académie Goncourt who had been invited to Giverny.

The new studio was some 75 feet long by 43 feet wide and 50 feet high, and while the dimensions suited Monet's requirements, he lamented its ugliness, referring to it as "that horrible thing." In a letter to

ABOVE: *Monet photographed in the third studio by Henri Manuel. The walls are lined with*
the Grandes Décorations *that the artist always planned to have exhibited in an oval room. The*
glasses with an opaque left lens placed on the table indicate that this picture must have been taken
after Monet's cataract operation in 1923. OPPOSITE: *On a small table lie boxes of the pastels*
that Monet used intermittently throughout his career, often while he was away on painting trips
waiting for his canvases to arrive, and sometimes as a simple change from oil painting. The white
china cat that Monet liked to keep on his couch was a present from a Japanese visitor.

ABOVE: *On a July afternoon in 1915, Monet sits beneath an immense parasol on a high chair in front of his easel, painting a weeping willow. Blanche stands at his side. After Alice's death in 1911, she took over the running of the house, looking after the artist and accompanying him on his painting expeditions.*

RIGHT: *Monet would spend hours contemplating this private world of shadow and reflection. The waterlily paintings were to become increasingly abstract: recognizable landmarks such as the river bank, bridges, and horizon were gradually abandoned so that all that was left was the play of light and reflection on the surface of the water.*

Jean-Pierre Hoschedé in 1915, he even admitted to being ashamed of it. Spare and rectilinear, the interior of the building resembled a factory. The canvases were mounted on specially designed trestles on castors so they could be moved around easily. Yet in this functional space, magic resided in the glazed earthenware pots that held Monet's broad brushes and in the palettes bearing traces of ultramarine, cobalt, vermilion, ocher, dark green, and rose, the pigments that satisfied his appetite for color.

The problem of heating such a large space during the war, when resources were scarce, was solved by Monet's friend Clemenceau, who was Prime Minister of France at the time. He introduced the artist to the Minister of Commerce, Etienne Clémentel, who arranged for supplies of coal and vast quantities of oil paints and large canvases to be sent to Giverny.

The working area was lit by an enormous skylight, over which a white linen shade was drawn when required to simulate the changing effect of natural daylight. The system of iron trusses meant that there was no need for additional roof supports.

Monet worked in the large studio for ten years. Throughout that period, he continued to be dogged by difficulties. He was depressed by the war and the thought of the suffering of the fighting men; this anxiety was compounded when his son Michel was sent to the front. Monet's eyesight also continued to deteriorate: by 1923, it was so bad that he agreed to an operation to remove a cataract on his right eye. An immediate improvement in his sight was then followed by new symptoms: the colors he saw did not remain the same but changed as he looked at them, an appalling problem for a painter who sought to reproduce the subtle shifts of light and tone in the natural world. The deaths of many of his old friends, Mirbeau and Geffroy among them, left him feeling isolated, though the devoted care he received from Blanche, Alice's daughter and the widow of his son Jean, sustained his

energy and artistic ambitions.

Despite his age and increasing frailty, he continued to paint until a few months before he died at the age of eighty-six, working not only on his *Grandes Décorations,* but also on smaller pictures of the Giverny flower garden. His bequest to the French nation, the

ABOVE: Waterlilies, *c. 1922. Twenty feet long, this vast panorama is purged of any precise reference to the site, so that the viewer is plunged into a world of waterlilies and reflections of sky and foliage.*
OVERLEAF: *The poolside planting was carefully planned by Monet to provide a perfect frame for the expanse of water that became his chief subject.*

twenty-two panels of his Waterlily cycle, found a permanent home in Paris six months later when they were installed in the Orangerie of the Tuileries. The public response was mixed, as Monet had himself predicted when he wrote, "They may get used to it, but I have come too early."

VIII

Monet's Bedroom

As part of his modifications to the original barn, Monet created a small suite for himself above the studio drawing room. The bedroom was light and airy, with two large south-facing windows overlooking the garden and a wide picture window facing due west, which caught the rays of the setting sun. Described by Gustave Geffroy as "a museum," it was filled with his private collection of pictures by his friends and by other painters he particularly admired. The adjoining dressing room, with its large armoire and washstand, also had a door into Alice's dressing room and a window overlooking the garden.

LEFT: *The painted mirror frame is decorated with strips of ovoli molding. At the top and bottom, loosely knotted bows of carved ribbon catch up garlands of laurel leaves intertwined with fruit and flowers.*
RIGHT: *When visitors came, the bed was covered with a huge ivory-colored cashmere shawl with a colored border. The fine linen sheets were embroidered with Monet's initials, and the pillowcases were edged in lace.*

THE PALETTE

Unlike the ground floor at Giverny, where everyone could walk through the house from one end to the other, the upper floor was a much more private area. Indeed, the only upstairs room that was occasionally open to visitors was Monet's bedroom, where a handful of friends were taken specifically to see the paintings that hung there. To offset his pictures and the few pieces of fine furniture he had acquired, he kept the setting simple.

The floor was of plain pitch pine boards, while wooden paneling with a dado rail covered the lower section of the walls. Above the dado, the walls were hung with wide strips of white damask cloth. These were sewn together to provide a uniform surface and bordered with a decorative edging.

An imposing fireplace of white marble veined in gray was surmounted by a huge mirror, placed partly to reflect the light and partly to create a

sense of perspective. Echoing the classical Greek lines of the fireplace and the Louis XVI mirror frame, Monet's bed was of the same style, its fluted corner posts, molded headboard, and feet painted off-white. Lying on his thick, well-stuffed woolen mattress, the artist had a good view out of the windows to the west and south and, using the sky over the hills as his barometer, could plan his day according to the weather before he left his bed.

LEFT: *For his correspondence, Monet used broad goose quill pens, which he cut himself. His roll-top desk also contained a traveling inkwell with Japanese-style decoration, a finely chased silver pen holder, and a dark green marble ashtray. In the many drawers of the desk, Monet kept his private and business letters, account books, and financial papers, from household bills to share certificates. The width of the top meant that there was also space for a few journals containing reviews of his exhibitions, and books on botany.*

RIGHT: *This detail of the pattern inlaid on the lid of the roll-top desk illustrates the exceptional talent of its mid-eighteenth-century maker, who combined a variety of hardwoods embellished with horn, tortoiseshell, gold, and silver to achieve his effects. Musical instruments and sheet music have been recreated down to the smallest detail.*

FAR RIGHT: *This cartel clock is made of painted wood and designed to be hung on the wall. The bronze ornamentation consists of fluid scrollwork and a little cupid perched on the top. Against the enamel face, the beautifully wrought hands show up as delicate as lace.*

Monet arranged the art collection in his bedroom deliberately to offer contrasts or to highlight similarities between the different works. He had a wide variety of paintings to choose from, including sketches by Delacroix and Boudin and landscapes by Pissarro and Sisley. There were also several Manet pastels, a Signac watercolor, twelve paintings by Cézanne, nine by Renoir, and several by Berthe Morisot, together with two Rodin bronzes.

In the early days at Giverny, Monet had not been able to afford good furniture. But once he was in a position to choose what he wanted, he showed discrimination in his purchases and selected some fine Louis XV and Louis XVI pieces. In their shape and decoration, these two contrasting eighteenth-century styles – the former infused with rococo exuberance, the latter more restrained and classical – represented the peak of French cabinetmaking.

Monet's superb Louis XV chest with gilded bronze mountings shows the influence of both Chinese art and the Italian baroque. It is decorated with marquetry in geometric patterns and varnished using a technique designed to imitate Far Eastern lacquerwork. Less obviously exuberant, the roll-top desk dates from the transitional period between the flourishes of Louis XV and the restraint and purity of Louis XVI. Probably the finest piece of furniture in the room, it is covered in a fine patterned veneer. It was here that Monet sat to write his letters when he was not using the studio drawing room. He kept in front of him one of the last photographs of Alice, taken on the Japanese bridge in 1910.

RIGHT: *From his bedroom window, Monet had a superb view over the long flowerbeds that run parallel to the Grande Allée, shown here in their late summer splendor, when the sunflowers come into their own and the beds are a riot of yellow and mauve.*

LEFT: *Although Monet was prepared to go out and paint in all weathers, there were days when the sky was too overcast. There were also times when he was assailed by doubts about his work. And at times like these he would become extremely bad-tempered, shutting himself in his room and even staying in bed all day. His moods affected the whole household, though the periods of bad humor were usually short-lived. On these days he took his meals in his room instead of the dining room. Alice or Blanche might bring up afternoon tea on a tray carefully laid with a silver teapot and a silver-bordered crystal cake dish.*

Monet kept his clothes in the dressing room adjoining the bedroom. Even as a penniless young man, he dressed stylishly: photographs of him at the age of twenty show a handsome figure in a striped vest, light-colored pants and a dark jacket. He wore his jackets with all but the top button undone, a fashionable practice of his youth which he kept to intermittently throughout his life. According to Renoir, he was known in Paris as "the Dandy" and was noted for the cut of his sleeves, his lacy shirt cuffs, and his skill in putting together his outfits. For despite his youthful poverty, Monet continued to order clothes from his tailor and fobbed off any requests for payment with claims that he could bring the man plenty of new custom from his growing circle of friends.

Over the years, he modified his sartorial style so it was firmly based on comfort. His whole wardrobe seems to have been chosen to give him freedom of movement no matter what the occasion. With such a varied life, he needed clothes that would take him anywhere. One moment he might be painting in the open air, the next entertaining visitors, or dining out in

Paris among the established names in the world of arts and letters. His travels covered the windswept cliffs of Normandy and the promenades of the French Riviera, as well as the chic Danieli Hotel in Venice and the London Savoy.

For the subtle synthesis of the country gentleman and the artist that became his preferred form of dress, he patronized a number of good tailors, including the Paris-based Scottish firm of Auld and Reekie. From them, he bought long, single-breasted jackets of tweed, alpaca, or cheviot wool, which were worn with wide pants tapering to the ankle above laced-up ankle boots. He also owned a number of three-piece suits.

Adaptable as these garments were, certain circumstances called for additional protection. In wet weather, he sported oilskins over a wide-rib sweater. The long-established Paris firm of Petit Matelot, or Little Sailor, supplied both the painter and the boys of the family with thick sweaters. In 1901, when he acquired his first car, a Panhard-Levassor, he bought a waterproof dustcoat to wear in it; and during the winter he kept himself warm with a fur-lined coat and cap.

ABOVE: *Monet's pride in his appearance did not not diminish in later years. In this photograph taken in 1897, he sports checked pants, a vest, fob watch, and cravat beneath a jacket fastened only by a top button, and one of his soft felt hats.*

OPPOSITE: *For the summer months, Monet had lightweight jackets and vests of unbleached cotton and linen, some with fancy patterns woven into the fabric. These were the clothes he liked to wear with a straw hat in the garden or on outings to the beach with the family.*

For his toiletry implements, Monet preferred brush-backs and combs made of old ivory and polished to an amber glow. On the shelves of the washstand, everything he needed for the cold bath he took in the early mornings was kept ready at hand, together with his shaving brush and soap and a pair of scissors to trim his beard.

THE PALETTE

Monet's dressing room was simply furnished with a sturdy washstand, a large mirror in a simple painted wooden frame, and a set of painted wooden cabinets for his clothes. The walls were painted soft blue, forming a muted background to the subtle colors of the Japanese prints that hung on them and the grayish mauve of the mirror frame.

Reflected in the mirror, the prints are predominantly depictions of the natural world. From Hokusai's series of Great Flowers, there are his famous *Chrysanthemums and Bee* and the *Peonies and Butterfly*. Hiroshige is represented by a *Crane* and by his gentle *Bird and Wisteria;* while Yoshitora's *Three Women in a Landscape with Flowers* seems to suggest the glories of the Giverny gardens.

Harmonizing with the mirror frame and with the grainy wood of the base below, the heavily veined marble of the washstand top has beveled edges and side panels carved in decorative curves. The central bowl was cleverly inset so that, in the days before main drainage was installed, it could be tilted so the dirty water could be emptied into a container hidden in the cabinet underneath.

Chrysanthemums and Bee, undated, Hokusai

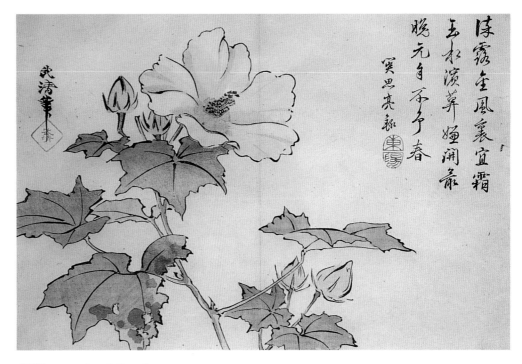

Hibiscus, undated, Busei

IX

Alice's Bedroom

Alice's sunny bedroom has windows on both the north and south sides of the house, giving views over the garden and across to the hills behind the village. In its unadorned simplicity, it is a far cry from a conventional nineteenth-century woman's boudoir and seems to have been planned specifically as a place to which Alice could withdraw from the bustle of the household for moments of contemplation on her own. It was here that she wrote her diary, did her correspondence, and kept the mementoes of her past life as Mlle Raingo and Mme Hoschedé, and her current role as Monet's companion.

Like Monet's suite, Alice's bedroom could be reached by way of the stairs leading up from the épicerie. It was also conveniently placed near the top of the main staircase in the entrance hall, which gave Alice easy access to the girls' rooms on the other side of the house and the boys' rooms in the attic.

The furniture here was probably ordered shortly after the family moved into the house in 1883. It came from a Paris department store, Les Grands Magasins du Louvre, where it featured in that year's catalog as a "varnished pitch pine bedroom set." Although the pine flooring, the bed, armoire, and tables are comparatively dark, the room itself seems light and bright. Sea-green walls and a matte white ceiling are enlivened by touches of glossy pastel blue on the baseboards, doors, and window frames to create an effect that is particularly pleasing when seen by candlelight. (There was no electricity in the house until 1909.) The same blue was used for the mirror frame over the dark mantelpiece.

To soften the apparent austerity of the plain furniture, Alice filled her room with items which had both decorative and sentimental value.

LEFT: *At night the room was lit by a pair of gilded bronze Louis XVI sconces, one on each side of the mirror, and two late-nineteenth-century Saxony faience candlesticks on the mantelpiece.*

RIGHT: *Unlike Monet, Alice kept her clothes in an armoire in the bedroom. During their initial period of hardship, Monet advised her to save money by buying her clothes ready-made instead of going to a dress-maker. But once she was able to indulge her taste for discreet luxury, she chose to be dressed by Worth. The large, richly colored cashmere shawl draped across the bed was one of the few things Alice took with her when she left the chateau at Rottembourg.*

THE PALETTE

Alice was a cultured woman from a comfortable middle-class background, who relished the good life and a respectable position in society. When her marriage to the wealthy Ernest Hoschedé ended in separation, it took courage to accept Monet's proposal that she and her six children move in with him, a penniless artist, especially as they were not able to marry until after Hoschedé's death in 1892.

The demands of running the large household at Giverny were considerable, and during Monet's frequent absences on painting trips Alice often felt abandoned, despite the fact that he obviously loved her very dearly. Nevertheless, she had a reputation for generosity and cheerfulness, and her diaries suggest that she was deeply religious.

Alice's keepsakes form a picture of a devoted mother and wife, and a lover of beautiful things. Among her collection of decorative watch cases were several engraved with the letter H for Hoschedé. She also owned some delightful miniature portraits of family members. Other pictures of the children were kept in photograph albums. Among the printed souvenirs was an invitation to the wedding of Alice's daughter Marthe and Theodore Butler. The couple married a year after Theodore was widowed by the death of Suzanne.

Monsieur et Madame
Claude Monet ont l'honneur
de vous faire part du Mariage
de Mademoiselle Marthe
Hoschedé, leur belle-fille et
fille, avec Monsieur Théodore
Earl Butler.

Et vous prient d'assister à la
Bénédiction Nuptiale qui leur sera
donnée le Lundi 31 Octobre 1900, à
11 heures 1/2, en l'Eglise de Giverny.

(Eure)

In the quietness of her room, Alice sat at her desk overlooking the flower garden and dealt with the practicalities of running the household, planning the menus both for everyday meals and for special luncheons. This was also where she wrote her letters. When Monet was away, she made it her business to keep him in touch with what was happening at home. Sometimes she would write of small domestic trials, a sick child or another child's poor exam results. When the girls were of marriageable age, she told him of any suitors in the offing. Occasionally, she would remind him of what he was missing, with descriptions of the garden. Monet's replies were full of words of encouragement, advice, and tender concern. In addition to sending "a thousand kisses" to everyone, he would issue detailed instructions about what was to be planted or transplanted before he got back, about picture frames that needed to be ordered, or about sending a note to the station master at Vernon to make sure he had a compartment to himself during a train journey from Marseilles to Paris.

This silent place was also where Alice confided her private confessions to her diary. She wrote in a good clear hand, setting down reminiscences and secret thoughts about the momentous events in her life. In this same small volume fastened with a clasp, her mother, Mme Raingo, had started keeping a diary after the death of her daughter Léonie. Thirty years later, in February 1899, Alice was recording her grief at the death of her daughter Suzanne after a mysterious illness. She was only 31, and left behind her husband Theodore Butler and two small children, Jim and Lily. Monet, ever the attentive husband, stayed at home to be with Alice and planned a few short trips, thinking they would help her recover. On one occasion, they drove to London with Germaine. In 1904 they traveled with Michel to Madrid and Toledo to see the collections of Velasquez and El Greco. Alice loved the speed of traveling in the car, and it had an exhilarating effect on her.

LEFT: *The view from Alice's bedroom window took in not only a broad sweep of the gardens, but also the balcony below.*
RIGHT: *In keeping with the simple furniture in the rest of the room, Alice had no antique desk to write at, but a small table just big enough to hold a scroll-patterned inkwell and a filigree letter-stand.*

The Japanese prints hanging in Alice's small suite were carefully chosen so their subject matter matched the intimacy of the setting. Most show women in a variety of private and public roles. Some are of European and American ladies going about their daily business in Yokohama, while others depict more delicate and sensual scenes of Japanese women at their toilette.

The work of Utamaro is well represented by a number of scenes of daily life: *Young Woman with a Mirror,*

Young Woman Smoothing her Hair in front of an Ikebana, c. 1804, Utamaro

The courtesan Aimi, undated, Toyokuni II

for example, *Young Woman with a Gauze Veil, Mother Playing with her Child,* and *Woman Emerging from her Bath.*

Together with these lively scenes of domestic activity, there are Kiyonaga's *Beauties* and *Courtesans,* stylized portraits of women so graceful and refined that they appear to have only one purpose: to seduce the viewer. Their eroticism always remains understated, conveyed merely in the curve of a neck or the smooth dome of a white forehead beneath elaborately dressed hair.

American Amusements, 1861, Yoshifuji

Portugal, 1861, Sadahide

Alice's dressing room was decorated in shades of green with pale blue doors. A wide mirror, its molded wooden frame colored to match the walls, was lit by a pair of candles on swivel brackets. Beneath the mirror stood a dresser with a pale marble top. The cut-glass bottles and jars with tops of the finest chased silver carefully arranged on its shelves reveal Alice as a fastidious and discerning woman, well versed in the secrets of feminine beauty.

Since freckles and tanned skin were frowned on in the late nineteenth century, respectable women like Alice applied the foundation creams and face powders required to create the velvety, snow-white effect then in vogue. Her cosmetics and scents were made by Rimmel, whose name is still used in France as a synonym for mascara. Like many women of taste, she favored light floral perfumes.

THE PALETTE

OPPOSITE: *Like her bedroom, Alice's dressing room was simply equipped with plain wooden furniture:*
a freestanding towel rack for the monogrammed towels, a cane-seated chair, a wooden dresser with a marble top, and an
oval china footbath. There were no closets because Alice kept her clothes in the bedroom.

BELOW: *Alice used beauty products based on light fragrances which were often named after the flowers from which*
they were made, such as orange-flower water from Grasse, powders scented with alpine violets, bath oil with tuberose, and white
lavender for massaging the skin. Cut-glass bottles and soap dishes, a nail buffer, a tortoiseshell comb edged with silver,
a swansdown powder puff, and tortoiseshell combs for securing a chignon were all essential to her toilette.

En Plein Air

At the height of summer, the scents and colors of the flowerbeds pervaded every room of the house. And in fine weather, the garden became the setting for the family's mealtime rituals. For summer lunches, when guests were frequently present, a striped awning was erected, big enough to shade a long table with a bench on each side from the glare of the sun. Afternoon tea was a full-scale ceremony: a table would be laid outside the studio drawing room and wicker chairs placed around it. Early evening cocktails were taken on the wooden balcony that Monet had added to the south front of the house.

RIGHT: *The double row of pleached lime trees between the main entrance and the studio drawing room provided shade for summer entertaining. This picture, taken in 1893, shows Monet's dealer Paul Durand-Ruel talking to the artist and his stepdaughter Suzanne in the foreground.*
LEFT: Monet's Garden at Giverny, 1895. *When Monet painted this view of a woman pausing in the Grande Allée to admire a bloom, the planting was well established. The colors were as carefully orchestrated as those in his paintings, and chosen according to the same principles of harmony and contrast.*

Monet was in the habit of strolling around his garden several times a day, checking on the progress of the plants and making sure that the gardeners were carrying out his detailed instructions. It provided him with a kind of spiritual refuge, and Arsène Alexandre observed the change that overtook him when he was lost in contemplation there: " This man who is laconic and rather cold in Paris is another person here – peaceful and enthusiastic. On the boulevards his smile is sardonic; in his garden among his flowers he is filled with happiness. The artist forgets that Paris exists for months on end ... The garden is the man."

Many of Monet's friends and guests were also keen gardeners who willingly compared notes and exchanged seeds or plants with him. Anyone who came to lunch would be conducted around the flowerbeds, water garden, and greenhouses afterward. Those who admired particular fruits and flowers often found that Monet sent them later as gifts, despatching the packages by train from Vernon.

Visitors would have walked from the balcony down the central flight of steps and straight into the Grande Allée, which ran the length of the garden. In 1920 Monet removed the cypresses lining the path, replacing them with flowerbeds and metal arches to support his favorite roses. This opened the vista out over the planting, whose profusion had previously been remarked on by Alexandre: "Everywhere you turn - around your feet, above your head, at chest level - there are lakes, garlands, and hedges of flowers, whose color harmonies are at once improvised, yet calculated, and which renew themselves each season."

One of the early improvements Monet made to his house was the construction of a balcony, which ran almost the entire length of the south facade. Freestanding trellises to support climbing plants, mostly roses, were added later. Monet's particular favorite was the large creamy yellow rose 'Mermaid,' which was planted below his bedroom window so he could enjoy its delicate fragrance.

ABOVE: *In summer the balcony became a place for entertaining, where everyone could enjoy the visual splendors and perfumes of the garden. This photograph shows Monet with three of Alice's daughters - Suzanne, Germaine, and Blanche - dressed in identical outfits, in accordance with the prevailing fashion.*

RIGHT: *When it was time for cocktails, rattan or wicker chairs were brought out from the studio drawing room and placed around the table. Visitors would be offered sparkling water, iced orangeade, cherry liqueur, a small port, or a measure of scotch accompanied by a few cheese straws or miniature meringues.*

RIGHT: *Afternoon tea was a carefully observed ritual. As a fitting complement to the far-eastern origins of tea, Alice chose to use her delicate Creil china, with its Japanese decorations. This was laid on a white embroidered tablecloth. Finely worked napkins and small silver spoons then appeared, along with a china teapot or one in pewter (the only metal that does not affect the taste of the tea). A selection of deliciously moist and delicately crumbly delicacies would be served. There might be scones, fruitcake and walnut shortbread, chocolate cake, and even miniature brioches, all of them homemade by Marguerite.*

CENTER: *At tea time, the ancient garden furniture was unfolded alongside the adults' tea table, and the children were served grenadine made from pomegranates along with homemade almond cookies.*

FAR RIGHT: *Alice's four grandchildren were also able to enjoy the garden. Because they were not allowed among the flowerbeds for fear of spoiling the blooms, Alice created a special play area for them under the lime trees, on one side of the house. Her granddaughters and their friends could play with their dolls, giving them tea in little tin cups with a Japanese design in imitation of the adults' tea party, or they might play in the improvised sandpile.*

When he first moved to Giverny, Monet brought a rowboat and two skiffs with him,
as well as the floating studio he used for painting on the river, which was specially adapted
with grooves in the floor to hold his canvases on stretchers. Boating became a family passion.
Jean Monet won prizes for his rowing, while Jacques Hoschedé grew up to become a
shipbuilder. The comparatively safe waters of the Epte also meant that the family could enjoy
swimming, diving, and fishing; Monet himself was a strong swimmer and often joined the
children for a dip. His paintings of girls boating testify to the pleasure that the family took in
the river. Boat at Giverny, c. 1887 (right), shows three of Alice's daughters - Germaine,
Suzanne, and Blanche - fishing from one of the skiffs, and other paintings show them rowing.
A similar boat to the one depicted in the paintings was used by the gardener to clear the
waterlily pond every morning before Monet began painting there (above).

Bibliography

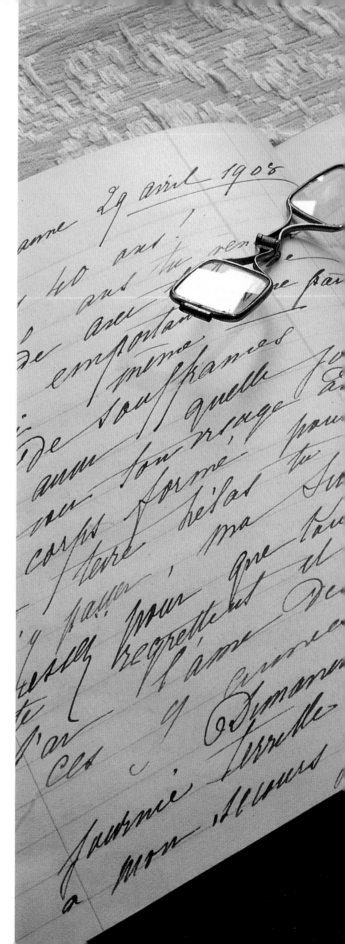

BOOKS

Aitken, Geneviève, and Delafond, Marianne, *La Collection d'Estampes Japonaises de Claude Monet* (Bibliothèque des Arts, Paris, 1987)

Alphant, Marianne, *Claude Monet: Une Vie dans le Paysage* (Hazan, Paris, 1993)

Clemenceau, Georges, *Claude Monet: Les Nymphéas* (Plon, Paris, 1928)

Fels, Marthe de, *La Vie de Claude Monet* (Gallimard, Paris, 1929)

Geffroy, Gustave, *Monet, sa vie, son oeuvre* (Crès et Cie, Paris, 1924, new edition, Macula, 1980)

Gerdts, William H., *Monet's Giverny: An Impressionist Colony* (Abbeville, New York, 1993)

Gordon, Robert and Forge, Andrew, *Monet* (Harry N. Abrams, New York, 1983)

Hackforth-Jones, Jocelyn, *A table avec les Impressionistes* (Adam Biro, Paris, 1991)

Hoschedé, Jean-Pierre, *Claude Monet, ce mal connu* (Pierre Cailler, Geneva, 1960)

Joyes, Claire, *Claude Monet - Life at Giverny* (Thames and Hudson, London, 1985 and Vendome Press, New York, 1985)

Joyes, Claire, *Monet's Table - The Cooking Journals of Claude Monet* (Simon and Schuster, New York, 1989)

Russell, Vivian, *Monet's Garden - Through the Seasons at Giverny*, (Frances Lincoln, London, 1995, and Stewart, Tabori and Chang, New York, 1995)

Tucker, Paul Hayes, *Claude Monet: Life and Art* (Yale University Press, New Haven and London, 1995)

Wildenstein, Daniel, *Monet, vie et oeuvre* (Bibliothèque des arts, Lausanne-Paris, Vol. I, 1974; Vols. II and III, 1979; Vol. IV, 1985; Vol. V, 1992)

ARTICLES

Alexandre, Arsène, 'Le jardin de Monet,' *Le Figaro*, August 9, 1901

Alexandre, Arsène, 'La Tamise, par Claude Monet,' *Le Figaro*, May 8, 1904

RIGHT: *Alice's journal on the desk in her bedroom.*
FAR RIGHT: *Books on the Louis XV chest in Monet's bedroom.*

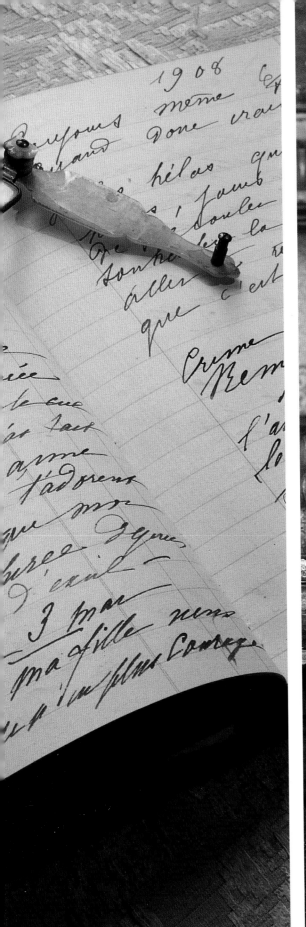

Index

Numbers in *italics* refer to illustrations and captions

VISITING MONET'S HOUSE

Monet's house and garden are open to the public between April 1 and October 31, every day except Mondays, from 10 A.M. to 6 P.M. On Mondays the house is closed but the garden is open to those wishing to paint. Appointments can be made by ringing the administrative offices on (02) 32 51 28 21; note that places are limited to ten people.

Giverny is 34 miles/55 kilometers northwest of Paris on the A13. The nearest station is Vernon, a one-hour train ride from the Gare Saint-Lazare in Paris. Since Monet's house is approximately three miles/five kilometers from Vernon, it is advisable to take a bus or taxi from the station.

AUTHOR'S ACKNOWLEDGMENTS

My thanks go to M Gérald van der Kemp, Member of the Institute and *Conservateur* of the Musée Claude Monet, Giverny; Mme Claudette Lindsey, Director of the Claude Monet Foundation, Giverny, and her colleagues; M Gilbert Vahé, Head Gardener at Giverny and his team; Mme A. Faÿ-Hallé, Director of the National Museum of Ceramics, Sèvres, for her wise advice; and the Japanese Language Institute. A special thank you must go to my friend Raphaëlle de Coninck, who helped with my research and to Joëlle Delaunay, who instinctively read between the lines I wrote, polished the text and transformed my handwriting into a faultless typescript.

Thank you to all those who generously lent some of the objects shown in the photographs; their kind collaboration has contributed much to this book: Au Bon Usage; Jean-Pierre de Castro; Eric Dubois; La Maison Fouquet; Fuchsia; Kimonoya; A L'Olivier; Au Puceron Chineur; Rubelli; Tanakaya.

PUBLISHER'S ACKNOWLEDGMENTS

The publishers would like to thank the Wildenstein Institute for permission to quote Monet's letters printed in *Monet, vie et oeuvre*, Ruth Carim and Maggi McCormick for their editorial assistance, and Helen Baz for the index.

PHOTOGRAPHIC ACKNOWLEDGMENTS

Photographic Styling Heide Michels
Artwork Joanna Logan
Editors Caroline Bugler, Christine O'Brien
Assistant Editor James Bennett
Editorial Director Erica Hunningher
Art Director Caroline Hillier
Picture Editor Anne Fraser
Picture Researcher Sue Gladstone
Production Peter Hinton